I0158651

Fortune Cookies

Volume 8

Dr. Kareem Pottinger

YSD Publishing House

Library of Congress Catalog in
Publication Data

YSD PUBLISHING HOUSE
14490 Coastal Bay Circle 13204
Naples, FL. 34119

Library of Congress Catalog Card
Number:
2013934185
International Standard Book
Number 978-1-937171-07-0

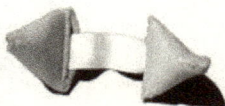

Dedicated to my firstborn

YOUNGSABATH POTTINGER

If I ever leave this planet, I have
always kept you in mind.

Not leavening my wisdom far behind

Grow Good

INTRODUCTION

The true intent of this book
was to write a set of guidelines
that could be
immediately implemented in
the progress and advancement
of my sons elite
life.
This vast deep knowledge was
to be used as a
tool
to keep him far beyond just,
"ahead of the learning curb" for
lack of better expression.
These
rules are the widely accepted
and used unspoken
secrets amongst the elite in
which we use to rear our

young.
Although these are our
secrets
and most of us will and should
be extremely displeased for
having them on display for the
"normal's" of the world to
receive, I decided to release
them nevertheless.
For,
upon reading the finished
piece I realized that these elite
secrets
could not only serve to benefit
my son and family to come
well, but that the entire
world
could serve to benefit from
these lists of guidelines.
The way that this book is
intended to be received is to

ponder upon each page for a complete 24 hours.
Each page is to be pondered upon for the whole day; it is to be used as topic of discussion for that day amongst peers, friends, and family members' etcetera.
It is especially designed to be pondered upon mostly by you. For a complete 24 hours deep thought on each subject should be pondered upon. The reason being is to see how these guidelines could be implemented into your current life, how should they have been implemented in your past life, and how can they benefit your future.

It
is only through the true
belief
and usage of these
guidelines
that your life's
works will be greatly
affected
in its progress.

1

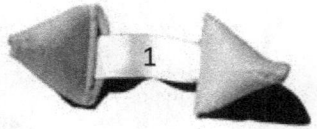

*People get
inspired
by the things
that are
around them
which
is why you
should
surround
yourself around
things that are
great*

When you
still
remember,
it makes it
that
much
harder
for
you
to
fully
forgive

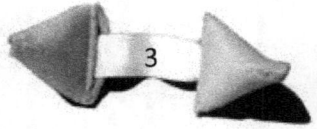

Diversify;
you
shouldn't
like
to
put
all
your
eggs
into
one
basket

4

*Do not be so
focused
on where you
are placing
your feet
that you don't
look-up
to see the
things
that are
around
you*

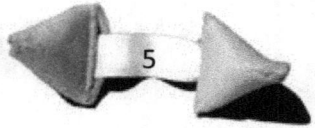

You
can have
everything
you
want in
this life,
if you
follow
your head
and
not
your heart

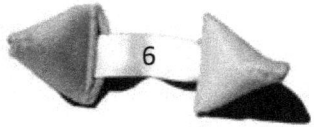

Downwards
may
sometimes
be
the
only
way
forwards

*Small
steps
towards
your
goal
is
better
than
no
steps
towards
your goal*

*You should
never
show
a
thing
before
it
is
ready
to
be
shown*

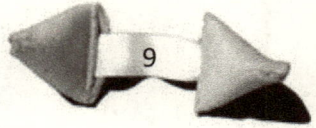

*You
have to
get-off
of
your
bottom
in
order
to
make
a
buck*

*When drawing
a conclusion;
it is very
wise
to keep in mind
that the
passing of
time
does change
your view on
certain
situations*

*Goals
give your life a
sense of
direction
and when you
don't have a
course plotted
your just going
to end-up
staying in the
same
position*

You have to learn how to live life according to life's rules and when you do, you will see how simple things become

*One of the
secrets
to
success
is
image,
adjust
your image
and
you will
adjust your
success*

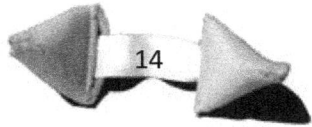

*What you
believe
and
decide
is
right
for you,
is not
for someone
else
to
decide*

Try things your way; you were put here on earth for a reason

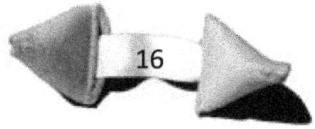

*It's
always
an
excellent
idea
to
elevate
perfection*

What cannot be done alone, can be done together with the help of others

18

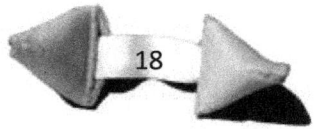

*It
is
very
important
to
know
how
to
change*

*Remember
that when
dealing
with business-
people,
it is all about
the
money
and the
rest
is just
conversation*

Time changes everyone including your friends

21

In the things that are worth your efforts, you have to see it all the way through

*The
distance
between
genius
and
insanity
is
measured
only
by
success*

*Do
not
make
a
problem
where
there
isn't
one*

The people in your life that do not make you happy should be considered like the weeds in your garden

On
a
road
made
of
"if's",
there
are
few
second
chances

*Learning how
to put
things
behind
you
and to do the
job
that you are
suppose
to do,
is
key*

*Sometimes
it
takes
an
inconvenience
to
put
you
into
the
proper
perspective*

*Everything
that
happens,
happens
how
it
has
been
set-up
to
happen*

*No effort that
you put forth
towards
a goal
is ever lost,
whether
small or
large it all
accumulates
into
your
achievement*

*Define
your
own
goals
and
you
will
become
your
own
person*

31

*When
in
the
spotlight,
you
can not
make
simple
mistakes
like
everyone
else*

*What
you
want
and
what
you
need
are often
on
two
different
pages*

*When you learn
to see
yourself
how other
people see
you,
then you will
begin
to get a grasp
of what your
true value
is*

*In
all
your
worthwhile
agendas,
never
give
up
hope
on
yourself*

35

Everything

gets

illuminated

in

the

light

of

the

past

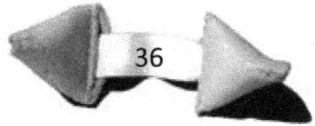

It's

amazing

the things that

you

can get

accomplished

when

you

don't

have

a

choice

*It
is
very
important
to
know
your
partner's
true-intent*

Upon trying to accomplish your desires you have to be smart about the goals you set

*Hope
always
works
out
when
given
a
chance
to
take
root*

*We
cannot
become
what we
need
to
be
by
remaining
what
we
are*

*Realize
the fact that
you
can't
please
everyone,
but
you
can
always
please
yourself*

*There is no way
around doing
what you
have
to do
in order
to get
where
you
have
to
go*

*Whatever
doesn't
sit
well
with
your
common-sense
should
not
be
believed*

*To give
your
best-shot
every
single
time
is
the
true
definition
of
brilliance*

44

*The
quick-fix
will
always
be
here
today
and
gone
tomorrow*

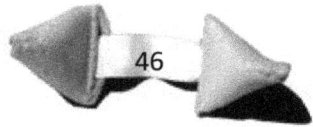

*It
is
easy
to
pass
someone
when
their
driving
in
reverse*

*The
real
essence
of
beauty
is
peace*

*We cannot all
share paradise
because we
don't all
deserve to;
some people
will not
arrive
and maybe
some of them
you will be very
close to*

*In life not only
is it
important
to know
when it is the
time
to change
but
you must also
have
the courage to
change*

*You have
to
believe
when you
want
to
achieve,
only
then
can
you
achieve*

*Your
job
as a
leader
will
always
be
not
to
screw
things
up*

You
should never
give-up
on your
life and the
things that you
are doing
in order
to help
others,
not even for a
moment

*When
you
learn
how
to
improvise
you
can
live
through
anything*

*Purposeful
steps;
each
one
of
your
steps
in
life
should
be
purposeful*

Every person has a price they will willingly accept, even for what they hoped never to sell

There
comes
a
time
when
you
must
take
responsibility
for
your
own-actions

How do you get
from
where you
are
to where
you
want
to be,
should
be
your
main-concern

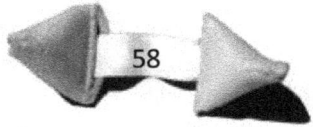

*People
have
many
different
reasoning's
for
doing
the
things
that
they
do*

59

When you do everything all at once; you're bound to lose something, which is why it is important to accomplish things piece by piece

In
life
many
things
are
a
marathon
and
not
a
sprint

Do everything

you can

to

put

forth

your

best-effort

and

you

can

accomplish

anything

*With
each
choice
you
make, either
a
new-destiny
is born
or an
old-one
is
reassured*

*In life you have
to make sure
that the
path
that you are
currently on
does not take
away from or
destroy the
possibilities
of your
future*

When

your

unsure

it

doesn't

hurt

to

ask

After all your work, it is that little moment in which you succeed that makes everything worthwhile

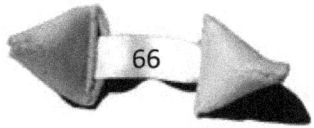

*We are
all
responsible
for our
own-lives
and
the sooner you
learn
that, the faster
your goals can
be
accomplished*

*Mixing
social
and
professional
is
a
terrible
combination*

*Upon
making your
assessments,
do not get
surprised
when you
realize that
people
can
be
very
stupid*

*Sometimes
the
end
of
everything
is
just
the
beginning
of
it
all*

*It
takes
a
true
friend
to
stab
you
in
the
front*

*In order
to
accomplish
anything,
you have
to have the
want
and you also
have to
put forth
the
effort*

*Never
forget
that
all
the
others
can
be
replaced
by
others*

*Always
remember that
you were
put here
on
earth
to
enjoy
living
and
not to burden
yourself*

*Unless they
change
their train of
thought,
the rich
will always be
rich
and the poor
will
always
be
poor*

*If
you
never
reach
for
anything,
you'll
never
have
anything*

*It
all
has
to
start
from
somewhere,
so
get
started*

In order to continue advancing levels and to keep up with the progress of progression, it is more about the things you have to do rather than the things you have already done

*Upon
applying
maximum
effort, just
remember that
you can
only
do
what
you
can
do*

*Miracles
have to be
worked
upon,
you
can't
expect
them
fresh
from
the
start*

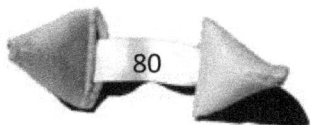

When
you
mess
with
a
bull,
don't
forget
that
it
has
horns

*An
oversight
will
come
back
to
haunt
you*

*Over
modification
can
weaken
any
structure*

*At some point
in your
life
a
clear-choice
must
be made as to
where
or
how
to
proceed*

*It's
not
always
the
most
popular
person
that
gets
the
job
done*

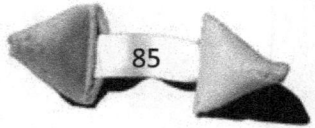

Anything
is
obtainable
with
the
proper
belief,
dedication,
and
efforts

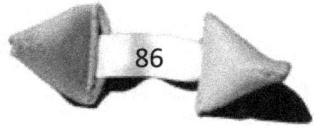

*Love
is
a
thing
that
is
built
on
communication
and
attraction*

*Maximum
value
should
be
your
big
picture*

*You
have to
have
balance
in
a
relationship
or
it
becomes
a
dictatorship*

*Regret
is
usually
a
waist
of
time,
do not
involve
yourself
in
it*

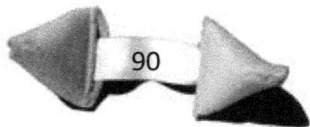

*Don't
over think
it,
you either
jump
in
with
both
feet
or
you
don't*

91

*A marriage
could
be
very
hard
work
if
both
aren't
pulling
their
weight*

*You have to
be-careful with
things
because
they
do
develop
a
momentum
of
their
own*

93

Every friendship has its peaks and valleys

*You should
never
force
yourself
into
a
mold
that
isn't
you;
be
yourself*

*You will be
unable to
blossom
into your
fullest potential
if
you are
unwilling to
venture of into
unknown
or
new-territory*

*More
is
lost
from
indecision
than
by
wrong
decision*

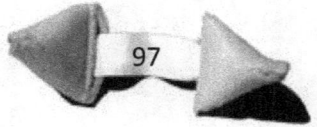

Let
sleeping-dogs
lie
or
they
will
bark,
with
the
potential
to
bite

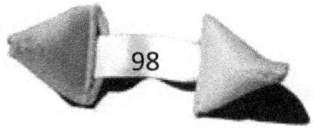

There
comes
a
time
where
you
must
recalibrate
your
course

*Learn
not
to
take
comfort
in
other
peoples
words*

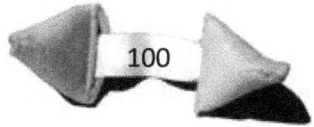

Sometimes

you

get

only

a

choice

of

evils

to

choose

from

You cannot kill a memory

*People
will attract
to you
when
they can see
that you
are
doing
something
with
your
life*

103

*People
will do
things
to you
that you
would
not
conceive
of
for
your
money*

In
life
you
will
win
some
and
you
will
lose
some

*Remember that
it is possible
for people
to
take
a
different
perspective
from
the
same
situation*

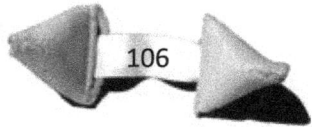

*There
will
always
be
doubters
in
life,
it is very
important
not to
listen to
them*

Any one
can oppose;
it's fun to be
against things
but
there comes a
time in life
when you have
to start
being
for
things

*Those
who
do not
like you
can be placed
into
two categories;
either the
stupid
or
the
envious*

*When dealing
with
people always
remember
that
some peoples
picture frame is
too small in
order to
comprehend
the
bigger picture*

When
right
is
right,
it
will
always
be
right

The heart wants what the heart wants, until ready it cannot be helped

*In life you
should always
try to
be
the
best
possible
you that you
can
be
at
all-times*

*No-one
on
the
receiving-end
really
likes
an
experiment
of
interest*

*Your
life
will
carry
out
at
your
own
expense*

*Any
partnership
is
give
and
take*

*In life you have
to
present
yourself
to
people
the
way
you
want to
be
treated*

*Do not
depend on
other
people
to make
you
who
you are
or
want
to
become*

You cannot evolve without taking risk

*A person
that
wants
to
succeed
in
a
great-way
has
to
have
large-plans*

When opportunity comes knocking the smart person answers

*In every
relationship
the
person least
interested
in
maintaining the
relationship
is going
to be
the
dominant-one*

*When
you
cannot
find
a
way,
you
have
to
make
a
way*

The
universe
does
not
make
mistakes

*When
you
repeat
something
enough
times
it
starts to
become
apart
of
you*

*In
competition;
the
only
thing that
really-matters
is
the
size
of
your
heart*

*We
all
have
our
own
cohesive-roles
to
play
on
this
planet*

To
settle
for
being
happy
is
a
trap

When you're clever enough you can get away with anything

Stand
in
a
fire
and
you
will
be
consumed
by
that
fire

In regards to dealing with yourself; you should never take a short-cut

*At
the
end
of
it
all,
you
get
what
you
deserve*

*Those people
who live up
there in the
clouds
are not
above
pushing each
other off
so that they
can
stay
up-there*

*"Hell"
is the
time
that you
should
have
left,
when
you
didn't*

*It is important
for you
to
keep
in mind
that
each person
in life
is on
their
own
journey*

*Don't
let
anyone
confuse
you,
you
never
get
something
for
nothing*

*Once
you
start
with
bad-habits
the
way-out
is
very
difficult*

*Always
go
straight
for the
top,
it is the only
way
you are going to
make
something
substantial of
yourself*

When your thought-process is set in the motion of; one-step closer to a better life for yourself and a brighter future, you will always end-out on top

*You should
always
stay
with
what
works
for
you*

*When you have
many
options
to
weigh
and a lot of
decisions
to make,
keeping it
simple
always works
best*

The biggest part of judging character is knowing yourself

No matter how much you advise someone, they will never truly-learn until it happens to them

You should always want something more from your life

*Youth
is
equivalent
to
endless
possibilities
so
make
great
use
of
it*

*When
the
universe
puts it
in your
heart
to do a thing,
then
you
should
definitely
do that thing*

*Never
make
your
own
life's
pieces
a
manipulation
for
someone
else's
gain*

*Rushing
things
allows
for
the
quality
of
certain
aspects
to
go
down*

*In life you have
to be
careful
of
spending
too much
time
on
things
that really
do not
matter*

You
are
in
control
of
your
own
story,
no-one
else

*When you fail
to look
at the
bigger picture,
it
becomes
impossible to
know
the
consequences
of your
actions*

*Your past
will
always
shape
the way
how
you feel,
perceive, and
think
about
the
future*

Everything that
you
do
towards
your goal
will put
you
one-step
closer
to
accomplishing
your goal

The issue in life
that
you may often
times
have; is that,
can
you run fast
enough
to
keep-up
with
everything

*What
is
your
model
of
upward
mobility
or
do
you
even
have one*

In
order
for things
to
run-smooth,
sometimes
you
have
to
make
the
"nice"

You have to
break-down
to the
fullest even the
simplest
of their actions,
to know
exactly
what type of
people you
have
around you

You

have

to

feed

your

mind

in

order

to

gain

intellect

*In
life; in
anything that
you do,
you
should
always be
concerned
about a
little-thing
called
indiscretion*

*There is no
need to
awake
a
sleeping
issue
especially
when
it
has
already
been resolved*

The end

Additional books written by
Dr. Kareem Pottinger available online at

www.FORTUNECOOKIES.me

and your local book stores nationwide

<u>FORTUNE COOKIES VOLUMES 1-11</u>

also available on your

<u>Kindle</u> <u>Nook</u> <u>Apple</u> <u>devices</u>

  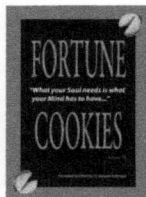

www.ingramcontent.com/pod-product-compliance
Lightning Source LLC
Chambersburg PA
CBHW030104070426
42448CB00037B/952